Straight Forward with Science

THE EARTH IN SPACE

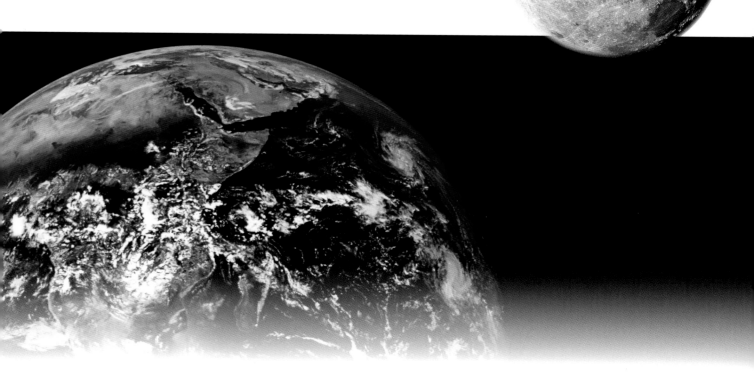

Peter Riley

W

FRANKLIN WATTS
LONDON•SYDNEY

To my granddaughter, Tabitha Grace

First published in Great Britain in 2015 by The Watts Publishing Group

Copyright text © Peter Riley 2015
(Text has previously appeared in *Straightforward Science: The Earth in Space* (2003) but has been re-written for this edition.)

HB ISBN 978 1 4451 3557 1
Library ebook ISBN 978 1 4451 3556 4
Dewey classification number: 520

Editor: Julia Bird
Designer: Mo Choy Design
Illustrations: Sebastian Quigley/Linden Artists and Peter Bull

Printed in China

Photo acknowledgements: angelinast/Shutterstock: 7c. B.A.E. Inc/Alamy: 27t. blickwinkel/Alamy: 24b. Norma Cornes/Shutterstock: 22t. Marvin Dembinsky Photo Associates/Alamy: 28r. Design 56/Shutterstock: 2, 16b. Designua/Shutterstock: 16c, 17b. ella1977/Shutterstock: 7cr. Johan W Elzenga/Shutterstock: 15b. Bill Frische/Shutterstock: 3, 6t. godrick/Shutterstock: 22b. Horizon International Images/Alamy: 12t. industryandtravel/Dreamstime: 19b. jdwphoto/Shutterstock: 15t. JTB Media Creation/Alamy: 7t. Korinov/Shutterstock: 4. a.v.levy/Shutterstock: 14b. manjik/Shutterstock: 12b. Mel Manser Photography/Shutterstock: 20, 31. NASA: 5b, 10t, 11t, 28l, 29b. NASA/JPL/Caltech: 18l. Timothy Passmore/Shutterstock: 21b. PF-(space-1)/Alamy: 8. pjmorely/NASA/Shutterstock: front cover, 1. RGB Ventures/Superstock/Alamy: 11b, 26t. Vasily Smirnov//Shutterstock: 26b. Stocktrek Images Inc/Alamy: 10b, 14t. Universal Images Group /Alamy: 29c. Wrangel/Dreamstime: 25t.

Every attempt has been made to clear copyright. Should there be any inadvertent omission, please apply to the Publishers for rectification.

Franklin Watts
An imprint of
Hachette Children's Group
Part of The Watts Publishing Group
Carmelite House
50 Victoria Embankment
London EC4Y 0DZ

An Hachette UK Company
www.hachette.co.uk

www.franklinwatts.co.uk

FSC
www.fsc.org
MIX
Paper from
responsible sources
FSC® C104740

Contents

What is space? 4

Stars 6

The Solar System 8

The inner Solar System 10

The outer planets 12

Space rubble 14

The moving Earth 16

The Earth and sunlight 18

The Sun in the sky 20

The Moon 22

Eclipses 24

Investigating space 26

Life in space 28

Glossary 30

Index 32

About this book 32

What is space?

When you look up into the sky, you are looking into space. It begins about 100 kilometres above your head, but nobody knows where it ends. The Sun and other stars and planets, including Earth, are all found in space.

❚ As you look up into the night sky, any clouds are in the atmosphere (see below). The Moon, planets and stars are in space.

THE ATMOSPHERE AND SPACE

The air we breathe is part of the atmosphere. This is a mixture of gases which forms a layer over the surface of the Earth. The Earth's gravity pulls the gases towards it. About 1,000 kilometres above the Earth, the force of gravity becomes too weak to pull the gases any longer. This is where the atmosphere ends and space begins. In space, it is dark and cold. There is no air, but there are clouds of gas and dust.

THE BIG BANG

Many scientists believe that about 13.8 billion years ago there was a huge explosion called the Big Bang. After the Big Bang the universe formed. Most of the universe is made up of dark, empty space, but it also contains billions of stars. The Big Bang began at a small point, no bigger than the dot on this 'i', after which the universe expanded in all directions. It is still expanding today.

The Sun

I The Milky Way Galaxy has a spiral shape.

GRAVITY AND THE STARS

Gravity acts between objects in space. It pulls them together or makes them move round each other. It pulls particles of matter together to make stars. The stars cluster in groups called galaxies. There may be hundreds of billions of stars in a galaxy and there are over a hundred billion galaxies in the universe. The Sun and planet Earth are found in the Milky Way Galaxy.

I This photograph is a very deep view of space. It shows hundreds of galaxies. The colour of a galaxy is used to estimate its age and distance. Bluer galaxies contain young stars and may be closer. Redder galaxies contain old stars and may be further away.

Stars

Most of the lights in the sky, including the Sun, are stars. A star is a huge ball of gas that is constantly changing, giving out heat and light.

WHY STARS SHINE

A star is made from two gases – hydrogen and helium. At the centre of a star, the force of gravity is so great that it pushes hydrogen atoms together to form helium atoms. As this change takes place, large amounts of energy are released. They pass through the star and escape from its surface as light and heat.

WHEN STARS DIE

Stars do not last forever. Eventually they all run out of hydrogen. When a yellow star like the Sun dies, it swells into a large red star, then shrinks and cools to form a white dwarf star. Eventually, it changes into a black dwarf star and stops shining for good.

EXPLOSION

Larger stars collapse as their hydrogen store runs out. If the star collapses very quickly, it explodes and forms a super nova. This gives out huge amounts of light and dust. The gravity of the remaining material at the centre of a super nova is so strong that not even light can escape from its surface, and a black hole forms.

A star is formed when gases in a huge gas cloud, called a nebula, are pulled together by gravity.

1. When a yellow star runs out of hydrogen it swells up and cools down.

2. As it cools, it changes colour to red. The large red star is known as a red giant.

6

▌The Southern Cross is a constellation that can only be seen in the southern hemisphere.

CONSTELLATIONS

Almost all the stars we see in the night sky are in the Milky Way Galaxy. They are really at different distances from the Earth, but they seem to be grouped together. These groups are called constellations. Each one is named after the shape it makes in the sky. The people who named them lived long ago and named them after objects, animals and gods.

▌The constellation of Orion can be seen in both hemispheres.

▌The Great Bear constellation can be seen in the northern hemisphere. This part of it is called the Plough.

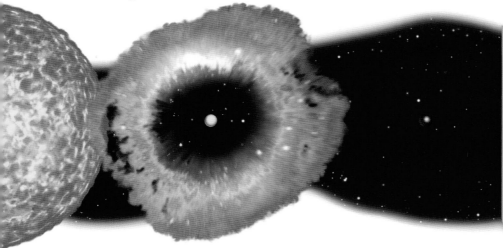

INVESTIGATE

Look for constellations in the night sky. Start by looking for one of the constellations in the pictures. Are all the stars in a constellation the same brightness? Are they all the same colour?

3. Later the star shrinks and loses gas and dust into space. It becomes a white dwarf star.

4. Eventually the star stops giving out light. When this happens the star becomes a black dwarf star.

7

The Solar System

The Sun is a star. It did not form at the beginning of the universe. It formed from a cloud of gas and dust made by other stars. This cloud also formed the other objects around the Sun. We call the Sun and the objects around it the Solar System.

HOW THE SOLAR SYSTEM FORMED

About 4.6 billion years ago there was a cloud of gas and dust in the Milky Way Galaxy. It measured about 1.5 million million kilometres across. A star exploded nearby and sent shock waves rushing through the cloud. The shock waves pushed on the cloud and made it turn round and round and form a disc. The gases and dust inside the disc swirled round its centre. Most of the hydrogen and helium collected at the centre of the disc and formed the Sun – a yellow star.

Neptune

▌The Sun formed around 4.6 billion years ago.

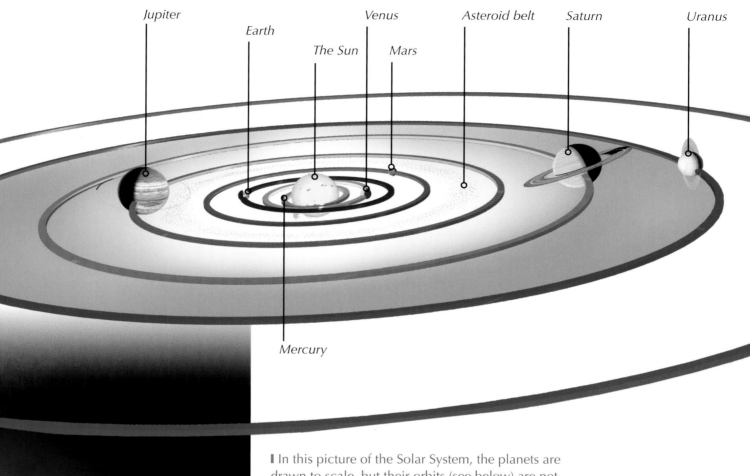

Jupiter

Earth

The Sun

Venus

Mars

Asteroid belt

Saturn

Uranus

Mercury

▌In this picture of the Solar System, the planets are drawn to scale, but their orbits (see below) are not. Jupiter is the biggest planet. Mercury is the smallest.

THE PLANETS

After the Sun formed, most of the remaining gases and dust became spinning spheres of matter called planets. One of these planets is the Earth. Each planet travels in a path around the Sun called an orbit. Between the orbits of Mars and Jupiter a band of rocks called asteroids formed into a belt surrounding the Sun (see page 14).

INVESTIGATE

Stars twinkle, but planets shine steadily. Look for a planet in the sky, such as Venus and Jupiter which are white and Mars which may look slightly red, and see it change position every night.

The inner Solar System

The planets in the Solar System can be divided into two groups – the inner planets and the outer planets. The orbits of the inner planets are inside the asteroid belt. All the inner planets are made of rock and some of them have moons that move in orbit around them (see page 22).

MERCURY

Mercury is almost 58 million kilometres from the Sun. It has a thin atmosphere containing hydrogen and helium. It rotates about once every 59 Earth days and completes its orbit in 88 days. The daytime temperature reaches 430°C and the night time temperature drops to −180°C. The diameter of Mercury is 4,879 kilometres – just a little larger than our Moon. It does not have a moon.

VENUS

Venus is about 108 million kilometres from the Sun. It has a thick atmosphere of carbon dioxide with clouds of sulphuric acid. Venus rotates once every 243 Earth days and completes its orbit in about 225 Earth days. Its atmosphere traps the Sun's heat and the surface of the planet averages around 465°C. The diameter of Venus is 12,104 kilometres. It does not have a moon.

❚ The surface of Mercury is covered in craters.

❚ Venus has many volcanoes and is covered in lava.

EARTH

Earth is almost 150,000 million kilometres from the Sun. Its atmosphere is mainly nitrogen and oxygen. The Earth rotates once every 23 hours 56 minutes and 4 seconds and completes its orbit in 365.25 days. Earth's temperature ranges from 58°C to –88°C and its diameter is about 12,742 kilometres. It has one moon, the Moon.

MARS

Mars is about 228,000,000 kilometres from the Sun. It has a thin atmosphere of carbon dioxide. Mars rotates once every 24 hours, 37 minutes and 22 seconds and completes its orbit in about 687 days. The temperature on the Mars equator in summer is 20°C, but it can reach –153°C at the poles. Mars' diameter is 6,785 kilometres. It has two moons.

 The Earth has large amounts of water. This has allowed life to develop.

INVESTIGATE

How does the temperature of the planets vary as you move from the one nearest the Sun to the one furthest away?

▌ Mars is red because it is covered in iron oxide – a substance commonly known as rust.

The outer planets

The four outer planets are known as gas giants. Under their atmosphere of hydrogen and helium are oceans of hydrogen, helium and other gases, such as methane and ammonia, that have turned into liquid. Below them is a rocky core. All of the gas giants are orbited by many moons and rings of dust and ice.

JUPITER

Jupiter is 778,500,000 kilometres from the Sun. It has a thick atmosphere of bands of clouds. It rotates once about every 10 hours and completes its orbit in 12 years. The temperature at the top of the clouds is −145°C but at the core it may reach 24,000°C. The diameter of Jupiter is about 143,000 kilometres. It has four faint dust rings and 67 known moons.

SATURN

Saturn lies about 1,433,000,000 kilometres from the Sun. It has a cloudy atmosphere, rotates once every 10 hours 39 minutes and completes its orbit in about 29.5 years. The temperature is −178°C on Saturn's surface and its diameter is 120,536 kilometres. It is surrounded by more than eight spectacular rings up to a kilometre thick. It has 62 moons.

❚ Jupiter's surface is covered in bands and swirls of clouds.

❚ Saturn's rings were discovered by the scientist and astronomer Galileo Galilei in 1610.

URANUS

Uranus is found about 2,870,000,000 kilometres from the Sun. Uranus rotates once every 17 hours 14 minutes and completes its orbit in 84 years. The temperature on Uranus can go down to –224°C and its diameter is 51,118 kilometres. It has 27 moons.

NEPTUNE

Neptune is about 4,500,000,000 kilometres from the Sun. It rotates once about every 16 hours and completes its orbit in almost 165 years. The average temperature on Neptune is around –224°C and its diameter is about 49,528 kilometres. It has 13 confirmed moons.

❙ Uranus and Neptune are blue due to the presence of methane in their atmospheres.

PLUTO

Pluto had been considered to be the ninth planet of the Solar System since its discovery in 1930, but the discovery of several similar icy bodies in the outer Solar System made scientists question Pluto's status as a planet. In 2006 Pluto was reclassified as a dwarf planet.

INVESTIGATE

How does the size of the gas giants vary as you move from the one nearest the Sun to the one furthest away? How do the rotation times compare?

Space rubble

After the Sun and the planets formed, there were many pieces of rock, icy chunks of frozen gases and particles of dust that continued to move through space. They formed smaller objects in the Solar System.

ASTEROIDS

Asteroids are lumps of rock that move in orbit around the Sun. Most asteroids orbit the Sun at a distance of 300–500 million kilometres, forming a rocky ring called the asteroid belt. Some asteroids are hundreds of kilometres across. Others are the size of a grain of sand.

❚ Asteroid 243 Ida is believed to be about 52 kilometres in diameter.

COMETS

A comet is a huge lump of ice and rock which moves in an orbit around the Sun. Billions of tiny particles leave the Sun every second and move through space. They form the solar wind. When a comet's orbit brings it close to the Sun, the particles in the solar wind push against the comet and a tail of gas and a tail of dust are produced. There are over 5,100 known comets, but there may be as many as a trillion in the outer Solar System.

❚ Comet Hale-Bopp, a very bright comet, could be seen from Earth with the naked eye for 18 months between 1995 and 1997.

❚ A streak of light made by a meteor can be seen here in the night sky.

METEORS

Meteors are small pieces of rock like pebbles, or the dust from the tails of comets. As the Earth moves along its orbit, these space rocks and dust are swept into the atmosphere.

Meteors rub against the gases in the atmosphere. This makes them heat up so much that they create a streak of light in the sky as they burn away. Another name for a meteor is a shooting star.

INVESTIGATE

Drop small stones into sand from different heights and compare the craters they make.

METEORITES

Meteorites are larger pieces of rock than meteors. They do not burn up when they enter the Earth's atmosphere, but instead fall to the ground. If a meteorite is large it can make a crater on the Earth's surface.

❚ This meteorite crater in Arizona, USA, is over a kilometre wide.

The moving Earth

As well as orbiting the Sun, the planets in the Solar System spin round, or rotate. Jupiter is the fastest rotating planet. It spins round once every 9 hours 55 minutes. The Sun also spins, taking 24 days to spin round once.

THE TILT OF THE EARTH

The Earth rotates once every 23 hours 56 minutes. It rotates on its axis. The axis runs through the centre of the Earth between the North Pole and the South Pole.

The level at which the Earth travels around the Sun is called its plane of orbit. The axis of the Earth is tilted at an angle of 23.4° to this plane. The Earth remains tilted at the same angle and pointing in the same direction as it moves round in its orbit.

❚ The Earth's angle of tilt is measured from a line which is at right angles to the plane of orbit.

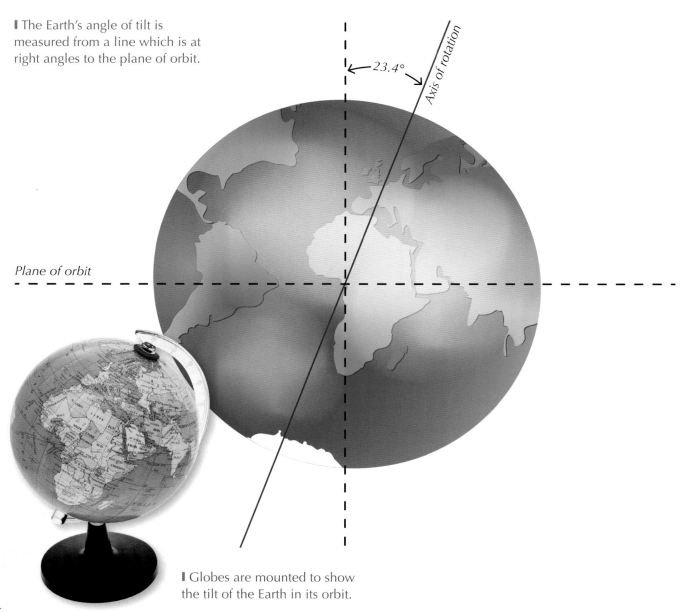

23.4°

Axis of rotation

Plane of orbit

❚ Globes are mounted to show the tilt of the Earth in its orbit.

MOVING IN ORBIT

All the planets are held in their orbit by forces of gravity. These pulling forces act between the Sun and the planets and between the planets themselves. The orbit is in the form of an oval, or ellipse. This means that there are two places in the orbit of a planet where it is closest to the Sun, and two places where it is furthest away.

The angle of the Earth's tilt means that the trajectory of the Sun in the sky varies over the course of the year. This gives us the different seasons (see pages 18–19).

(see pages 18–19)

INVESTIGATE

Attach one end of a string to a ping pong ball securely. Go outside and swing the ball around your hand. Pretend your hand is the Sun, the ball is the Earth and the string is the gravity between them. Find out what would happen if there were no gravity by letting go of the string.

▍ The position of the Earth in four places in its orbit. The closest points to the Sun are marked with a C and the most distant points are marked with a D.

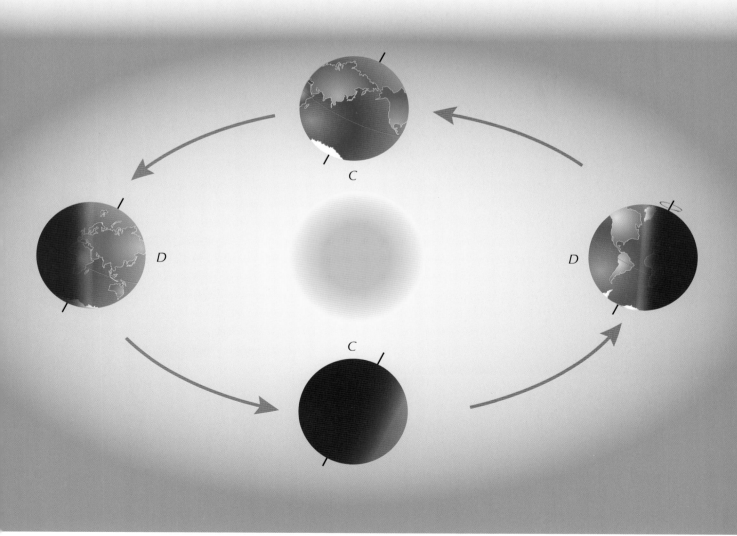

The Earth and sunlight

Only the half of the Earth facing the Sun is lit by sunlight. When one half of the Earth has sunlight, the other is in darkness. As the Earth rotates, almost every place on the planet has a period of day-time and a period of night-time.

I In this photograph, half the Earth and half the Moon are lit by sunlight.

SUMMER

As the Earth moves in its orbit, there is a time when the North Pole is tilted towards the Sun and the South Pole is tilted away from the Sun. When this happens, places close to the North Pole have 24 hours of sunlight and other places in the northern hemisphere have days with more hours of sunlight than hours of darkness.

When the Earth is at A, it is summer in the northern hemisphere.

WINTER

At the same time, places close to the South Pole have 24 hours of darkness and other places in the southern hemisphere have more hours of darkness than of sunlight. It is summer in the northern hemisphere and winter in the southern hemisphere.

TURN IT ROUND

As the Earth moves round in its orbit, the North Pole gradually comes to point away from the Sun and the South Pole comes to point towards it. This change makes the daytime shorter in the northern hemisphere and longer in the southern hemisphere. It is summer in the southern hemisphere and winter in the northern hemisphere. As the Earth moves on its orbit, daylight lengthens in the northern hemisphere and shortens in the southern hemisphere. At a place halfway between the summer and winter positions in the orbit, the poles neither point to or away from the Sun. At this time it is spring in the northern hemisphere and autumn in the southern hemisphere. Six months later when the same conditions occur again it is autumn in the northern hemisphere and spring in the southern hemisphere.

When the Earth is at B, it is summer in the southern hemisphere.

B

▍A sign marking the equator in Kenya. The equator is always pointing towards the Sun. The length of day does not change here, and the weather does not get hotter or colder, but stays very hot.

KARIBU KENYA!

EQUATOR

HAKUNA MATATA

19

The Sun in the sky

When the day begins, the Sun rises over the eastern horizon. During the day, the Sun moves across the sky until it sinks beneath the western horizon. In all this time, the Sun has not really moved in space. It is the rotating Earth that makes the Sun appear to move.

THE RISING AND SINKING SUN

At any one place on Earth, the Sun rises in the sky in the morning because the place is turning towards the Sun. At midday, the place is facing the Sun directly and the Sun is at its highest point in the sky. From midday until sunset, the place is turning away from the Sun and the Sun appears to sink in the sky.

▌In the morning the Sun appears to rise above the horizon.

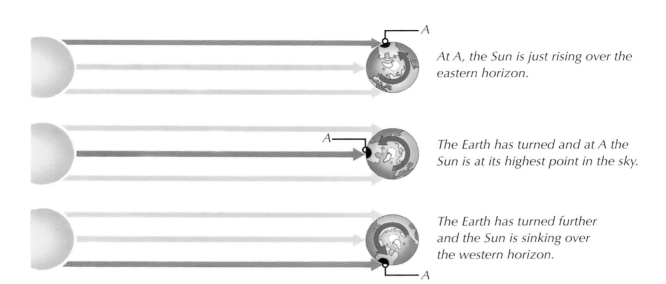

At A, the Sun is just rising over the eastern horizon.

The Earth has turned and at A the Sun is at its highest point in the sky.

The Earth has turned further and the Sun is sinking over the western horizon.

SHADOWS AND TIME

As sunlight shines on objects on the ground, the objects cast shadows. At the beginning of the morning, the shadows are long and point towards the west. During the morning, as the Sun rises, the shadows become shorter and point towards the north in the northern hemisphere and towards the south in the southern hemisphere. In the afternoon, as the Sun sinks, the shadows become longer again and point towards the east. The position of the Sun and shadows have been used for thousands of years to measure time.

INVESTIGATE

Set up a pencil on modelling clay in the middle of a piece of white paper. Mark the pencil's shadow each hour through the day. Use your sundial over the next few weeks and see how the shadows change. [**Warning**: never look directly at the Sun. It can damage your eyes.]

❚ The time of day can be told from a sundial by looking at the position of the shadow.

The Moon

At night when the Sun has gone down, the Moon shines in the sky. The Moon is the Earth's natural satellite. It orbits the Earth while the Earth orbits the Sun.

WHAT IS A MOON?

A moon is an object made of rock that moves in an orbit around a planet. It may be spherical like the Earth's Moon, or have a more irregular shape like the two moons of Mars.

❚ The Moon does not create its own light – it reflects light from the Sun.

THE TURNING MOON

The Moon is only about a quarter of the Earth's size. It orbits the Earth at a distance of only 384,400 kilometres. It takes 29.5 days to travel around the Earth once.

The Moon rotates slowly as it moves in its orbit. It rotates with the same speed as it orbits the Earth. This means that it always has the same side facing the Earth.

❚ The Moon's surface is covered in mountains that look white and dusty plains that appear grey.

THE PHASES OF THE MOON

The amount of the Moon that is lit up in the sky depends on its position in orbit. One side of the Moon is always fully lit but it is not always the side facing the Earth. If the side that is fully lit is facing away from us, our side of the Moon is dark. As the Moon moves in its orbit, we can see more of its fully-lit side. First we see just a small part of it and the Moon is called a new moon. Eventually the whole of the fully-lit side is facing the Earth. This is called a full moon. These changes in the Moon's appearance are known as the phases of the Moon.

INVESTIGATE

Try to draw the Moon every night for a month. Compare your pictures with the phases of the Moon on this page.

❙ This diagram shows eight positions of the Moon in orbit around the Earth. The outer ring shows how the Moon looks from the Earth in each position.

new moon

full moon

Eclipses

Once every orbit, the Moon is the same side of the Earth as the Sun. When this happens, we do not see the Moon because our side of the Moon is dark and the Sun is bright in the sky. The Moon is also usually in a different part of the sky from the Sun. If it was in the same part, it would cover up the Sun's light.

AN ECLIPSE OF THE SUN

Every few months, the Sun, the Moon and the Earth line up. If this happens when the Moon and the Sun are in the same part of the sky, the Moon comes between the Earth and the Sun. This is called a solar eclipse because the light of the Sun is eclipsed, or covered up.

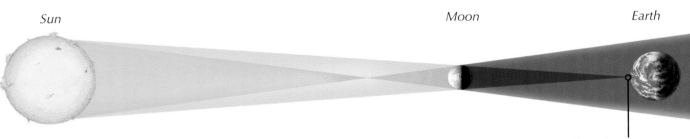

Sun *Moon* *Earth*

Eclipse can be seen from here.

❚ During a solar eclipse, the dark Moon moves in front of the Sun.

AN ECLIPSE OF THE MOON

Sometimes the Sun, the Earth and the Moon line up with the Earth in the middle. When this happens, the Earth stops the light of the Sun from reaching the Moon. Without the light of the Sun, the Moon stops shining. This is called a lunar eclipse because the Moon appears to have been covered up. During a lunar eclipse, the shadow of the Earth passes across the Moon until the Moon is covered up.

▌During a lunar eclipse, the light of the Sun cannot reach the Moon and make it shine.

Sun   *Earth*   *Moon*

The Moon moves into the shadow of the Earth during a lunar eclipse.

TOTAL AND PARTIAL ECLIPSES

A total eclipse of the Sun, where the Moon totally covers the Sun, can only be seen from a small area of the Earth as the diagram on page 24 shows. From other parts of the Earth the Moon is seen only to cover part of the Sun. This is called a partial eclipse of the Sun.

A partial eclipse of the Moon occurs when only part of the Earth comes between the Sun and the Moon. The Earth then casts a shadow over just a part of the Moon's surface.

INVESTIGATE

Use a globe, a tennis ball and a torch to demonstrate the eclipse of the Sun and the Moon. For the eclipse of the Sun, move the tennis ball between the globe and the torch. For the eclipse of the Moon, move the globe between the tennis ball and the torch.

Investigating space

The first investigations of space were made by mapping the constellations. Telescopes allowed more stars and planets to be seen. The invention of rockets allowed spacecraft and probes to make investigations out in space which continue today.

TELESCOPES

Telescopes provide a way of looking at things that are very far away. Some telescopes collect light rays from space, others collect radio waves. Most telescopes are on Earth, but there are also telescopes in orbit around the Earth. The telescopes in orbit can collect light and radio waves from deep space.

❙ A technician prepares the Kepler Space Telescope spacecraft for launch.

SPACECRAFT

A spacecraft carries scientific equipment or astronauts into space. It has to travel very fast to break free from the pull of the Earth's gravity and enter space.

When spacecraft reach space, they usually move in orbit around the Earth. Some spacecraft are designed to move out of orbit and explore other places in space.

❙ Spacecraft are launched on the top of powerful rockets that carry them away from the strong pull of the Earth's gravity.

INVESTIGATE

Use the Internet to learn about the latest investigations taking place in space.

I NASA's *Curiosity* robotic rover has been used to investigate the surface of Mars.

SPACE PROBES

A space probe is a spacecraft which carries cameras and scientific equipment such as thermometers. It may also carry robot vehicles to explore the surface of other planets. The space probe sends the information it collects back to a space centre on Earth.

When a space probe reaches a planet, parachutes open to let it slowly sink to the planet's surface. As the probe descends, it collects information about the planet's atmosphere.

I The Huygen probe is the most distant space probe to land in another part of the Solar System. It investigated the atmosphere of Titan, a moon of Saturn, as it descended to the moon's surface.

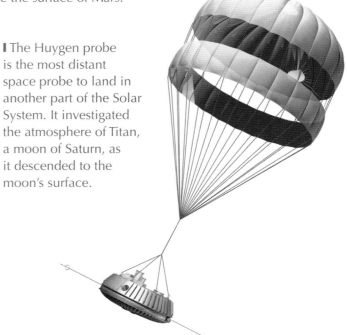

Life in space

Conditions in space are very different from conditions on Earth. Without special protection, astronauts would only survive there for a few seconds. Despite these problems there are plans for people to work on the Moon and to visit Mars.

SURVIVING IN SPACE

Space travel presents many challenges. Humans need to breathe oxygen to stay alive. Oxygen is one of the gases in the Earth's atmosphere. In space there is no atmosphere, which means there is no oxygen to breathe. The Earth's atmosphere also protects us from harmful ultraviolet (UV) rays and X-rays given out by the Sun. Temperatures in space can vary from 121°C to –156°C. Humans cannot survive at these temperatures.

A spacecraft protects astronauts from space's conditions. They are kept comfortable by life-support systems which provide oxygen, remove carbon dioxide and dampness, and prevent the air from becoming too hot. When astronauts are outside the spacecraft, they wear spacesuits which provide them with all the systems they need.

❚ In the past, astronauts have visited the Moon. More may do so in the future.

❚ Astronauts move around on the outside of spacecraft to carry out repairs and set up experiments.

WEIGHTLESSNESS

When a spacecraft is high above the Earth, gravity pulls it around the planet. The orbiting spacecraft and everything inside it behave as if they did not have any weight. This condition is called weightlessness. Everything inside the spacecraft can float freely in the air. Weightlessness makes the muscles and bones become weaker so astronauts have to exercise regularly to keep them strong.

❚ These astronauts can float in the spacecraft easily. At mealtimes, their food can do the same thing!

SURVIVING IN SPACE

There have been many spacecraft missions to take astronauts into space. In 1998 the International Space Station (ISS) was built. Astronauts can live there for many months as they carry out a wide range of scientific investigations. These include examining changes on the Earth and in the structure of the universe. The weightless conditions also allow new ways of investigating disease-causing microbes and cancer treatments, as well as the development of new materials and machinery such as robotic arms for use in brain surgery. There are also investigations into the effect of space travel on the human body, such as changes in muscles and bone, which will help to prepare astronauts for future space missions.

Glossary

ammonia – a chemical with a strong smell.

asteroid – a piece of rock that is in orbit around the Sun. They vary in size from the size of a grain of sand to 940 km across.

atmosphere – the layer of gases that surrounds the Earth.

axis – the imaginary line around which a planet turns. The north and south poles of a planet are at either end of its axis.

Big Bang – the explosion which occurred when the universe began.

black hole – part of a collapsed star which has such a strong force of gravity that light cannot escape from it.

carbon dioxide – the gas that we exhale.

comet – a large lump of rock and ice in orbit around the Sun that produces two tails when it is near the Sun.

constellation – a shape made in the sky by a group of stars.

crater – a hollow on the surface of a planet or a moon made by a rock falling on it from space.

diameter – the length of a straight line across the middle of a circle or sphere.

Earth – the third planet from the Sun. It has a diameter of 12,742 km. It rotates once in about 24 hours and takes 365.25 days to orbit the Sun. The Earth has one moon.

equator – an imaginary line around the middle of the Earth. The equator divides the northern hemisphere and the southern hemisphere.

gravity – a pulling force between any two objects in the universe. Gravity causes objects to fall to Earth and stops everything on Earth from floating off into space.

helium – a gas that is lighter than air and is used in party balloons.

hydrogen – a gas that is lighter than air and produces an explosion when set on fire in the air.

International Space Station – a space station which orbits the Earth. Astronauts from many different countries live there for up to a year at a time, carrying out experiments and research.

iron – a type of metal. When iron gets damp, some of the iron atoms combine with oxygen atoms to form iron oxide (rust).

Jupiter – The fifth planet from the Sun. It has a diameter of about 143,000 km and rotates once in about 10 hours. It takes 12 Earth years to orbit the Sun. Jupiter has 67 known moons.

Mars – The fourth planet from the Sun. It has a diameter of 6,785 km. It rotates in just over 24 hours and takes 687 Earth days to orbit the Sun. It has two moons.

Mercury – the closest planet to the Sun. It has a diameter of 4,879 km. It rotates once every 59 Earth days and takes 88 Earth days to orbit the Sun. It has no moons.

meteor – a small piece of rock from space which gets close enough to Earth to be pulled towards it. A meteor burns up in the Earth's atmosphere.

meteorite – a large piece of rock from space which gets close enough to the Earth to be pulled towards it. A meteorite does not burn up in the atmosphere, but falls to the Earth's surface where it may make a crater.

methane – a gas which on the Earth is used in cookers and central heating systems.

nebula – a cloud of gas and dust in which stars may form.

Neptune – the eighth planet from the Sun. It has a diameter of around 49,528 km. It rotates once every 16 hours and takes almost 165 Earth years to orbit the Sun. It has 13 confirmed moons.

orbit – to travel around something in space.

oxygen – a gas in air that humans need to breathe in order to live.

particle – a very small part of something.

probe – a robotic spacecraft that explores space.

radio waves – waves of energy that can pass through space and the atmosphere and carry information.

rocket – a machine which burns fuel and produces a jet of hot gases. The force of the gas jet moving out of the back of the rocket is balanced by a pushing force which moves the rocket in the opposite direction.

rover – a space vehicle used to explore the surface of the Moon or Mars.

Saturn – the sixth planet from the Sun. It has a diameter of 120,536 km. It rotates once in 10 hours 39 minutes and takes 29.5 Earth years to orbit the Sun. It has 62 moons.

telescope – a device which makes distant objects seem closer than they really are.

thermometer – a piece of equipment that measures the temperature.

ultraviolet (UV) rays – invisible, but very powerful, rays of energy given out by the Sun. Exposure to too much UV light can damage your skin.

Uranus – the seventh planet from the Sun. It has a diameter of 51,118 km. It rotates once in 17 hours 14 minutes and takes 84 Earth years to orbit the Sun. It has 27 moons.

Venus – the second planet from the Sun. It rotates once in 243 Earth days. It takes 225 Earth days to orbit the Sun. Venus has no moons.

volcano – a mountain which has a tube called a vent. Through the vent materials from inside the planet can escape onto the planet's surface or into its atmosphere.

X-rays – a form of electro-magnetic radiation given off by the Sun and other stars. X-rays can pass through parts of the human body and are used to build up a picture of bones and some organs.

Index

ammonia 12–13
asteroids 9–10, 14
astronauts 26, 28–29
atmosphere (of planets) 4–5,
     10–13, 15, 27–28

Big Bang 4

carbon dioxide 10–11, 28
comets 14–15
constellations 7, 26
Curiosity 27

Earth 4–5, 7, 9–11, 14–29
     day and night 18–19
     plane of orbit 16–17
eclipses 24–25
equator 19

galaxies 5–9
Galilei, Galileo 12
gas giants 12–13
gases 4, 6–15, 28
gravity 4–6, 17, 26, 29

helium 6, 8, 10, 12
hemisphere, northern 7,
     18–19, 21
hemisphere, southern 7,
     18–19, 21

holes, black 6
hydrogen 6, 8, 10, 12

International Space Station 29

Jupiter 9, 12, 16

Mars 9, 11, 22, 27–28
matter 5, 9
Mercury 9–10
meteorites 15
meteors 15
methane 12–13
Milky Way 5–8
Moon 4, 10–11, 18, 22–25, 28
     phases of 23
moons 10–13, 22, 27

nebulae 6
Neptune 8, 13
nitrogen 11
North Pole 16, 18–19

oxygen 11, 28

Pluto 13
probes, space 26–27

Saturn 9, 12, 27
seasons 17–19

shadows 21, 25
Solar System 8–9 (*and throughout*)
South Pole 16, 18–19
spacecraft 26–29
stars 4–9, 26 (*and see entries for Sun*)
     black dwarf 6–7
     red giant 6
     shooting 15
     white dwarf 6–7
     yellow 6, 8
Sun 4–14, 16–22, 24–25, 28
sundials 21
sunlight 18–21
super novae 6

telescopes 26

Uranus 9, 13

Venus 9–10

weightlessness 29

ABOUT THIS BOOK

This aim of this book is to provide information and enrichment for the topic of space in the Upper Key Stage 2 UK Science Curriculum. There are five lines of scientific enquiry. By reading the book readers are making one of them – research using secondary sources, and the investigations on pages 11, 13, 25 and 26 focus on this. The text is supported by simple investigations the reader can make to experience what has been described. Many of these investigations are simply illustrative to reinforce what has been read and practise observational skills, but the following investigations are also examples of types of scientific enquiry. Grouping and classifying: pages 7, 9; Pattern seeking: pages 7, 21; Observing over time: pages 9, 21, 23; Comparative test: pages 15, 17.